MUMMIES SECRETS OF THE PHAROAHS
Ancient Egypt for Kids
Children's Archaeology Books Edition

SPEEDY
PUBLISHING

Speedy Publishing LLC
40 E. Main St. #1156
Newark, DE 19711
www.speedypublishing.com

Copyright 2015

A mummy is the body of a person (or an animal) that has been preserved after death.

The afterlife
was an
important part
of Ancient
Egyptian
culture.

It was very important to ancient Egyptian religious beliefs that the human body was preserved.

In the Egyptian religion, the body was needed in order for the soul of the person to unite with the person in the afterlife.

They did this through a process called embalming.

The embalmed
bodies are
called mummies.

Ancient
Egyptians
started making
mummies
around 3400 BC.

The priests of
ancient Egypt
developed ways
to preserve
or 'mummify'
a body so that
it would last.

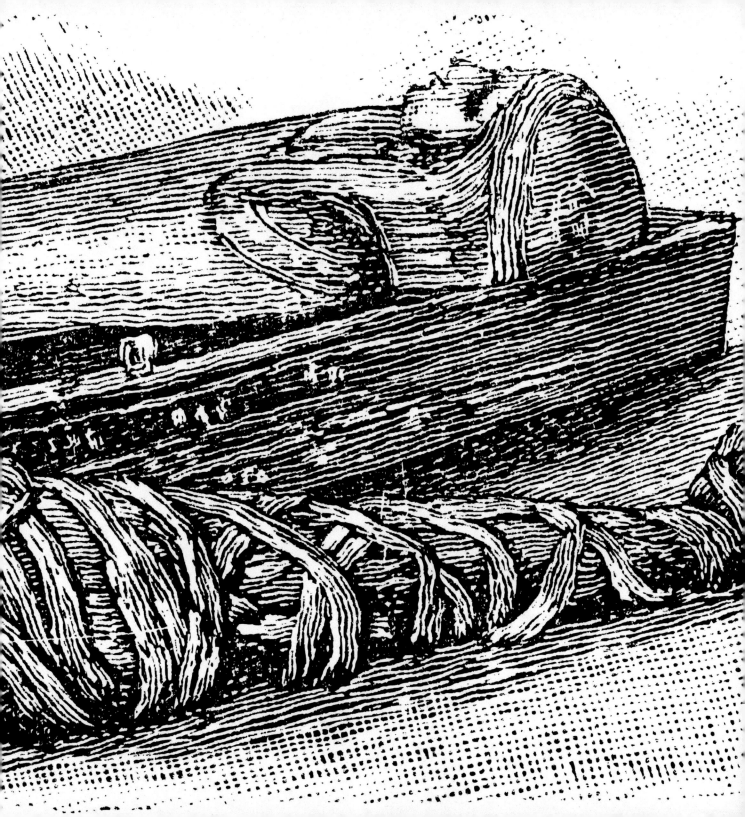

The mummies were any Egyptian who could afford to pay for the expensive process of preserving their bodies for the afterlife.

Pharaohs
had the most
expensive
mummification
of all people.

Since the pharaoh was considered a god they included many gems and amulets in between the layers of linen wrapping.

They would also use a special sarcophagus for the pharaoh that was carved and painted in his likeness.

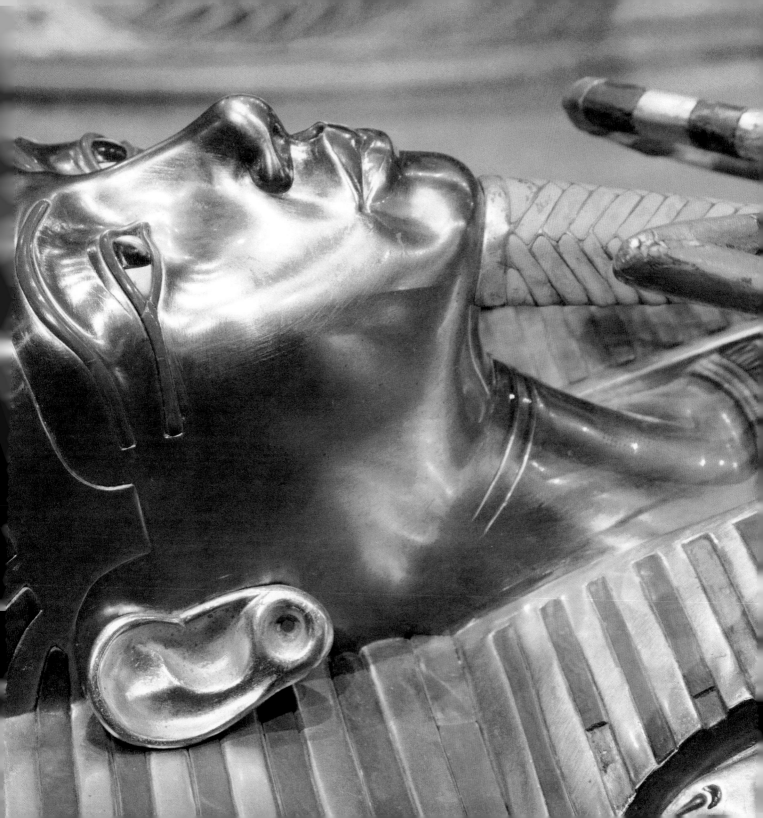

The pharaoh mummies were placed in special burial places along with many of the expensive items that they would take with them in the afterlife.

There were
special religious
burial rites
that had to be
performed
by the temple
priests at each
step of the
mummification.

It is estimated that 70 million mummies were made in Egypt over the 3,000 years of the ancient civilization.

The heart was left in the body because it was considered to be the center of intelligence.

Sometimes the mummy's mouth would be opened to symbolize breathing in the afterlife.

The pyramids are the stone tombs of Egypt's kings - the Pharaohs.

The tombs were designed to protect the buried Pharaoh's body and his belongings.

16216018R00024